CONTENTS

Preface	1
Title Page	5
Copyright	6
Chapter 1: What is Motivation?	7
Chapter 2: It's all your fault!	12
Chapter 3: There's No Such Thing as Trying.	16
Chapter 4: How to Deal with Stinkin' Thinkin'	20
Chapter 5: You Know How to Fix It	24
Chapter 6: You're on your Cycle	27
Chapter 7: Consistency is in You!	30
Chapter 8: I, Decided.	34
Chapter 9: Why?	37
Chapter 10: How to Have Faith	40
Chapter 11: Shut Up!	44
Chapter 12: What If	47
Chapter 13: Rest. Don't Procrastinate.	52
Chapter 14: The Racehorse Approach	56
Chapter 15: What's on the "Next Level?"	59
Chapter 16: Pizza vs. Oatmeal	62
Chapter 17: Be a FINISHER	66
Final Remarks	70

PREFACE

Message to the reader. This book is for people who don't know what they're next move is. People who often claim they lost motivation, didn't lose motivation, they had false expectations of it. You see, motivation is a feeling, not a mental state. It was only meant to get you started, not to help you finish, only dedication can do that.

This is not a self-help book. This book was written to teach you how to help yourself. It took me a year to write this book because I didn't want to write it with my talent. I lived it as I wrote it, so everything that you're going to read came from an organic place. No, fluff. No, games. I was excited when I wrote some chapters. I was angry when I wrote some chapters. I was nervous and afraid as to whether people would even buy this book. So, since you did let's get started.

I've become extremely fascinated with learning about what makes people quit. Quitting is the absolute worst thing you could ever do to yourself. While some are addicted to drugs, alcohol, and other horrible things. Some of us are addicted to quitting. Then we dress our quitting with the words, "I'm trying." I believe the old saying goes, "once you start stopping, you'll never stop". In just 30 years, I've learned this to be a true statement.

You see, I don't want this to become a "self-help" book for

you to read for a month and revert back to your old way of living. If you've picked up this book, it's because you've sought out yet another outside source of motivation. So, I guess the other books haven't helped much either. So, instead I'd rather challenge you to shift your entire way of looking at life. Once we truly commit to changing the way we think about ourselves, we become unstoppable. So, if you cry while reading some of the chapters in this book it's okay. If you become angry, frustrated, and disappointed in yourself as you turn the pages it's perfectly okay. We're going to dig deep into why you are where you are in life and with God's help, we're going to change your life from the inside out.

I have an amazing best friend in my son, Houston, he's eight going on 18. He taught me a valuable lesson about how people give up. When he was five, I decided to help him to learn to tie his shoes. He was so excited that I was going give this valuable know how. So, one day when we got home from church, we went into the TV room; I watched him with excitement as he untied his shoe laces. I went over the whole bunny ears routine with his laces over and over and over again, while he watched. No matter how many times I did it, he still couldn't seem to remember how to do it when it was his turn to try. Now, of course his Dad is big on not giving up, so, I told him that he could mess up as much as he needed to. The only rule was that he couldn't quit. I watched my son try for 30 minutes. Contrary to what people may assume about me, I'm really a softie when it comes to him. So, I gave him rubs on the head every time he failed. I watched all the stages of quitting happen in these 30 minutes. My son went from excited, to frustrated, to doubtful, to just plain helpless. I watched him try over and over until he decided that he couldn't win. My first instinct was to immediately force him to try until he got tired of trying. Instead, I looked him in the eyes and I said something I hope he remembers for the rest of his life.

If you're tired of trying, it's okay to rest for a while. Tomorrow's on the way and that's a new day to try this all over again.

You see I didn't force him to keep trying, but I didn't let him give up either. Your life is the same way. Along this journey you're going to have weak moments. Moments that make you feel excited, then frustrated, then doubtful, and then plain helpless. It's in those moments, that you must remember that you don't have to accomplish everything today. Tomorrow will get better if your mind tells it to. Now, before you start thinking I'm one of those self-proclaimed motivational coaches, let me stop you there. I've been down. I've lost careers because of bad decisions that I've made! I've made lots of money and then lost it all. But, one day I decided to get out of my own way. Start my mind over again and went on to create a seven figure business from nothing. And if I can do it, you can too.

Let's get started.

MOTIVATION IS AN INSIDE JOB

Finding the Motivation from Within

John Smith

Copyright © 2019 by John Smith

All rights reserved
Published in the United States by John Smith.

Cover Design by Daniel Jones
Edited by Sierra Rush
Book design by Sierra Rush

CHAPTER 1:
What is Motivation?

Motivation, dedication, and then transformation.

1

If you're reading this book that indicates that you're looking for motivation. This also means that you had it before, but you lost it. My objective in this book is to teach you what motivation is. What its purpose is and how to make it work for you; and not let the lack of it derail you.

Over the five years of me being a gym owner, I've become infatuated with the psychology of how people shift mindsets so quickly! We want better money, better bodies, better relationships, however, we don't know where to start. We ask ourselves questions like,

Am I able to do it?
Can I stick to it?
Why can't I seem to focus?

It's like everyone wants to change, but there's never been a blueprint on exactly how to. When I talk to my clients, I like to break it down into three phases: motivation, dedication, and then transformation. Each stage leads to the next so, let's go.

Most people think they lack motivation when it's really dedication that they lack. You've been looking at yourself in the mirror for weeks and weeks saying that you were going to change your diet. Yet you never do. The very fact that you hate your stomach means that you're motivated, it's that simple. Motivation is just a simple feeling that we give too much credit. If you want to succeed, you have to transition from motivation, to dedication.

See dedication is going to the gym when you really don't feel like it. Pushing through the frustrations of soreness. Denying yourself that bag of chips that you really want. Refusing the glass of wine, you think you deserve at the end of your work day by replacing it with water. Dedication is the hard part. It leads us, however, to transformation. Everything that transforms has to go through the dedication phase. Dedication is uncomfortable. Without this phase there can be no transformation. If you don't dedicate yourself to your gym for a long period of time, your stomach will not go away and you will remain at square one complaining and lying to yourself with the bull crap excuse, "I'm not motivated" so, let's explain these motivational phases.

Phase One: Motivation

I remember when my son was a baby and he could only crawl. When it was time for him to learn to walk I would stand him up and hold his toy a few feet away from him. He would take steps toward me, then try to grab the toy. Each time he failed, I would stand him back up and do it again and again. This is the motivational phase. When we see someone with a nice car or nice things or a nice body; and it motivates us to go after the same thing. So, just like Houston, we get up. We go to the gym or we decide to write that business plan or get our empire off the ground. Motivation is a great tool, but it's not the end all be all. Motivation wears off after a couple of weeks. That's probably why you can only stick to a diet for a couple weeks before reverting back to your old habits. This is why the next phase is so important.

Phase Two: Dedication

This is the next phase, which in my opinion is the most critical. Houston got tired of me having to standing him up and show him his toy. He became so obsessed with getting the toy from me that he eventually learned to crawl to a nearby couch or table leg and then he would stand himself up in order to attempt the steps yet again. Even though his legs weren't strong enough yet, he still tried. This is exactly what dedication is. Showing up and giving your best without someone telling you to.

Maybe the reason you haven't made it yet is because you're looking for every outside source to pick you up. It's not your trainer's job to make sure you eat right. It's not your pastor's job to make sure you live right. It's not your lawyer job to keep you from committing a crime. It's your job! They are all simply all just guides and support systems, but you have to do the work. Why would you want your friends, your family and your supporters to dedicate themselves to you and you won't even dedicate yourself to yourself. Dedication is a requirement, not an option. If you always wait for inspiration to do what you need to do, you'll never get anywhere in life

Phase Three: Transformation

When we hear the word transformation it makes us think of the physical. I would go on to suggest that the goal needs to be more mental than anything. In the Bible, it says that we should be transformed by the renewing of our minds. In other words, if your level changes before your mind does then it's only be a matter of time when you'll be back to where you started. I'm sure you know of people who had to get multiple weight loss surgeries because they kept eating bad after the surgery. When we want success without process we run the risk of becoming one hit wonders. No one wants to struggle anymore, no one wants to fight through any challenges anymore. A caterpillar can't get to the butterfly stage until it's endured the discomfort of the cocoon. Your mind is the cocoon. Either you can die there or you can develop. Everything that happens in your life, happens in your mind first. We'll discuss it more in the coming chapters.

CHAPTER 2:
It's all your fault!

You've lied to yourself for so long that you've actually started to believe that you can't get better.

2

That's right. I said it! Your fault! The harsh reality of life is that the quality of it lies in the bed of the decisions that we've made. We are all where we chose to be. You know why you're broke? Do you know why you're out of shape? Do you know why your marriage is falling apart? Do you know why you can't seem to stick to your diet? Well, go look in the mirror and you'll see the reason. YOU! You are the problem! As a matter of fact, I want you to say it out loud right now. No, no, no say it for real! Say it right now. Say it loud enough for your mind to hear it! You are your own worst enemy. Don't pass it on to others. Don't blame your parents for your upbringing. Don't blame your job for how they treated you. Don't even blame your ex for breaking your heart. YOU PICKED THEM! So, it's still your fault. The good news is that since you are your problem, you are also your own solution.

In this chapter I want you to admit your wrongs and apologize to yourself. You've lied to yourself for so long that you've actually started to believe that you can't get better. Today you're going to take a serious swing at this thing. After you've apologized in full. I want you to forgive yourself. Forgive yourself for not knowing how to get more for yourself. Forgive yourself for who and what you've become. You can lie to everyone else for who they think you are, but you can't lie to yourself.

You know when you haven't been giving 100 percent. You

know you could've done a better job. You know you could be making more money if you just went back to school. You know your wife wouldn't complain so much if you put in the little bit of extra effort she asked. Sometimes we confuse motivation with regret. We get so disappointed in ourselves sometimes, that it causes us to have a burst of speed in the other direction. However, it's one thing to change paths and it's another thing to change the habits that got us on that path. This is also why gyms are so packed in January, but empty in July. Which is also why divorce rates are at an all-time high right now. People give up so easily and quickly nowadays.

Your regret will frustrate you and it should. It won't carry you through your journey though. That pair of pants you can't fit anymore made you join a gym and if you didn't see your weight loss goal through that means you weren't really motivated. You were regretful at the moment. We don't regret decisions for long. We oftentimes try to mentally cope with them and bury them in excuses as to what got us here. The best thing to do is acknowledge why you are where you are and then you must devise a plan to ensure that you never return. So, let's dig a grave for your excuses right now.

After every chapter I want you to list some key notes to help you not just start a thing but to see it through. When you finish the book, I want you to look at your notes. Read this book as needed. Read it every month if you have to. If you find yourself getting mentally, emotionally or even spiritually weak, pick it up and let it remind you of who you are. Let's start here:

Questions:

List three areas that you've struggled with for some time.
1.

2.

3.

List three weekly goals to help you improve in these areas.
1.

2.

3.

CHAPTER 3:
There's No Such Thing as Trying

There's only doing and not doing…

3

Everyone who knows me knows I have a strong dislike for the word "trying". It's been said that the word "love" is the most loosely used and thrown out term that people use nowadays. However, I believe the most misappropriated word that people use these days is, trying. Here's my point. I want you to find a small object near you right now. Hold it in your hand. Now I want you to try to put it down, but don't fully put it down. Hold it in your hand and don't drop it, but, I want you to TRY to put it down. Make sure you put it down without dropping it out of your hand. It doesn't make sense to you either does it, that's because there's no such thing as trying. There's only doing and then there's not doing. Either you're going to eat right, or you're not. Either you're going to stop drinking or you're not! Either you're going to workout every day, or you're just going to continue to gain weight. Either you're going to save money or you're just going to go broke. It's always been your choice.

The word "trying" is a word used by the inconsistent to justify their laziness. It may sound harsh, but it's probably because you're not doing. Can you imagine how crazy you'd look if you "tried" to put on your shirt today but didn't fully put it on? People would think your nuts. So, why are you going through life every day giving 50 percent of your efforts? You don't become great until you BECOME great.

We live in a world where people want to get the most out

of life, and put the least in. Everything they sell on TV is a quick fix. "Get Rich quick! "File your taxes quick and easy!" Lose the weight by just working out just 15 minutes a day". None of that even sounds legitimate. The truth is a lot of people will never see their full potential in life because it requires a full level of sacrifice. Stop starting stuff that you're not willing to see all the way through. Quitting is going to cross your mind MULTIPLE TIMES on anything big that you set out to do. When it does, you have to be able to tell the difference between hardship and impossibility. What we often say we can't do is just what we don't want to do. Hardship has a way of wearing us all out sometimes. Come up with a way to keep your focus fresh. In order to do this, you have to stay focused on why you want what you want. Stop trying, and start doing.

Questions:

1. What has procrastination done to you?

2. How do you measure trying vs doing?

3. Look up the roots AND effects of procrastination stress and then re-answer question one.

CHAPTER 4:
How to Deal with Stinkin' Thinkin'

Adopt a mindset that looks at the positive side of things.

4

You ever had one of those days where you woke up, looked around your room, and just said to yourself, "I really don't feel like it?" Well suck it up, we all have. When faced with tough tasks that demand your immediate attention, immediately replace thoughts of frustration with thoughts of gratefulness. Positivity is a product of gratefulness. So, if you can't find your positivity, it's probably because you aren't grateful enough. While you're complaining about not wanting to go to work, there's a father who doesn't have a way to support his family. While you're complaining about not wanting to get up and go workout, there's someone somewhere in a hospital bed wishing for one more day. What gives you the right to complain? Who do you think you are? Do you understand that you woke up and saw another day? Stop pissing your life away with complaints and excuses that no one hears but you. It's time to wake up and take control of your life again. Frustration is real, but it's not going to help you think your way out of this.

Whenever I start to have negative thoughts I immediately think of how bad things could be. You may not have a car, but at least you have legs to walk to the bus stop. You may not live in the biggest house, but you're not sleeping outside. You may not have all the money in the world, but you had enough to buy this book to learn how to get you some. When you have thoughts that make you want to give up, replace them with thoughts that force you not to. The rise and fall of how we deal with tough times is called perspective. For as long as you live, you will have troubles. Adopt a mindset that looks at the positive side of things. I know most people say that positivity talk is kind of played out and easier said than done, but let me remind you of something. You will never be able to build something worth anything carrying a negative mindset. Progress needs positivity. If success is the goal, and progress is the car then positivity is the gas. There have been many days where I simply did not feel like being who I had to be. My choice of positivity outweighed my choice to be angry and frustrated. Now remember positivity shouldn't make you blind. If a man isn't treating you right, don't look for the positive in him so much that you ignore the reality of the situation. Here's a simple rule: When faced with a problem or bad situation ask myself, "Can I change it?" Or "Is there nothing I can do to fix it right now?" Because if I can change it, well there's no reason to be mad. I'll just change it and If I can't change it, then there's no reason to lose sleep over it! It's your thinking that got you where you are and if you're going to get out of the dark places of this level, you have to think your way out.

Question:

What are 3 major problems that you have right now in your life? Find a positive outlook for every problem you listed. Example "I don't have money for a new car but..."

1.

2.

3.

CHAPTER 5:
You Know How to Fix It.

No one's responsible for your wellbeing but, you.

5

I'm a firm believer that we all know exactly how to immediately make our lives better. We don't take the steps because of the stress that change requires. It's stressful to change. When you're new to a diet, you can't drink, you can't eat what you want and we are addicted to our coping mechanisms. Who do you need to stop talking to? What do you need to stop eating? What are you spending money on that has in you in a financial hole? See, you have an answer for every question I just asked. We don't like answering the tough questions because they require us to be truthful with ourselves and some people would rather live a comfortable lie than to deal with an uncomfortable truth. See truth hurts at first, but it eventually sets you free.

I remember my mom would plant flowers every spring, but she didn't just go out and plant the flowers. She would go get a tool from the garage and start turning the ground over. She would break up the old dirt that had gotten hard over the winter, so that the new plants could have fresh soil. If she would've planted those fresh beautiful fresh flowers, in the hard unturned ground, it would've killed what she was growing. Maybe the reason your stuff isn't growing is because you keep planting new opportunities in old ground. It's time to shake up some stuff. It's time to go after a new you and ladies I'm not talking about you going to get a new hairstyle. Why put new hair on a head with an old dirty - nasty perspective?

We have to look inward to see what we are doing wrong before we can change directions. Otherwise, we'll end up back where we started. No one's going to fix your life but, you. No one's responsible for your wellbeing but, you. Unless you have a spouse your destiny is on you and you alone. God gives you direction if you let him, but it's you walking on the water. You know what to stop spending money on. You know what you need to do to get your life right, so just stop! Now I know you may be asking yourself, "How in the heck does he expect me to quit the stuff I like so much???" Well I'm glad you asked.

CHAPTER 6:
You're on your Cycle

If you don't like something about your life, you must identify the thinking that got you there

6

This chapter is written to help you break your patterns. Where you are, is because of what you do, whether it has a positive or negative affect on your life, it's still true. If you don't like something about your life, you must identify the thinking that got you there. I'm sure you've washed clothes before, so you know how the machines work. Now when you take your clothes to the washing machine and you throw them in there, they get wet. When you put them in the dryer, they get dry. You can't put clothes in the washing machine, expecting them to get dry, simply because that cycle doesn't match that result.

Decisions lead to cycles. Cycles lead to results. Think about it, when you cheat your diet, you probably slip up around the same time every single day. You wake up with every intention on eating right. You get out of bed, you go look in the mirror at the body you don't like. You head to work determined to hit the gym, as your day progresses your will to will to win diminishes. The stresses of life drain all the effort you wanted to give yourself. You don't even have the energy to go home and cook; and then you whisper to yourself, "forget it, I'll try again tomorrow." Sound familiar? Well that cycle of thinking makes you wake up again the next morning, walk pass the same mirror and hate your body again. This makes you determined to eat right that day only to put it off again and again and again, until you start to say to yourself "I can't". When the truth is that you can, it's just that your goals aren't important enough to you yet. So, change your cycle. Pick a day to prep your food, make time to prioritize yourself even if that means waking up earlier. Remember there's no success without sacrifice, so don't be lazy. Changing the cycle is easier said than done, so you better have something to hold onto mentally.

Pray to God to help you with your consistency. Put your goal weight on your phone so you can see it again and again. You can even read this chapter every time you want to give in. When your work starts paying off it'll get easier and easier to commit. Trust me. If you want to change where you are, you have to change what got you here. You're never stuck. Don't confuse being stuck with being impatient with where you are. If you're working towards it then you're not stuck. You're only stuck if you quit. Great things take time.

CHAPTER 7:
Consistency is in You!

Make the weak areas of your life just as important to you as your successful areas

7

In the last chapter, we talked about changing cycles, redirecting thoughts, and deciding to become; now let's introduce you to the hardest part. Brace yourself, CONSISTENCY! Everyone gets excited to start these physical journeys these days, but very few actually make it to the finish line. In fact, only 2 out of 10 people actually stay focused to see their physical journeys through. Now, I'm sure all 10 people really wanted results; but it's the principle of consistency that draws the line of separation. There's a quote that sticks to me every time I hear it. I quote it to myself whenever I have weak moments. "We are who we are not because of what we say, but because of what we do." It's so funny how we can be successful in some areas and falter in others. For instance, how can you be a great businessman and a horrible husband? How can you strive at being a great singer but, you lack focus when it comes to your health? It's simply because our successful areas have structure.

Success requires structure. If you're reading this, then you're probably in some type of house or building. If you look around the room you'll notice that this building is held up by walls. What you don't see are the small nails and screws holding that structure together. Without these nails, it's impossible to keep the structure. If there are no nails there will be no building. Your consistency, your routine and your attention to detail are the little nails. If your diet sucks, marriage sucks, money sucks, credit sucks, or your business sucks it's probably because there's no structure in that area. There can be no long term success without structure. Here's the good news, if you've managed to show consistency in any area in life, then that means you have what it takes. You just have to redirect that same effort into your weak areas. Find a way to make the weak areas of your life just as important to you as your successful areas. Life is too short to go home every day the same way that you left. In fact, you should never go to bed until you're stronger, richer, smarter, and happier. Practice that principle daily and you're bound to progress in life.

When I view how people stay consistent it has nothing to do with, "how bad they want it." It has everything to do with how far they're willing to go to get the things we want out of life. I truly believe that we only prioritize what's actually important to us. Some people find more joy out of short term pleasures than they would seeking out a goal that will take some time. We'd rather drink or smoke to relieve the stresses of our lives. Now, these are temporary fixes. Temporary fixes often times lead to long term deterioration. Doctors don't put band aids on gunshot wounds, they have to repair it before they cover it. Most people who have drinking and substance abuse issues are masking something they've never addressed. That issue you're masking isn't going away. It's actually getting worse and worse the more you choose to ignore it, and if you don't address the wound in time you'll eventually bleed out. I'm not trying to be your therapist. I'm simply suggesting that maybe you should do something constructive about your issues that won't hurt you in the long term.

Whenever you see a construction process, the beginning phases are ugly. It's hard to see the beauty because there's so much dirt and debris everywhere. Over time, you see the construction crew moving the once scattered dirt and debris and blocks in a certain arrangement. As time progresses you see the building coming to life. After the brick and mortar are done they put the bells and whistles on everything. Well if you're at the beginning of your journey, expect the ugliness. It won't always be like this. Life has a way of helping us figure out where the dirt and debris goes. Over time, we put the blocks where they're supposed to go. The thing is, no one will be able to see the beauty of it but, you. Others will only marvel at the finished product. Stay consistent through the tough days; you're building something great.

CHAPTER 8:
I, Decided.

Nothing will happen for you if you don't make it happen.

8

Before we start I want you to do a quick exercise. Wherever you are right now, if you can, I want you to take both arms and reach as high as you can. Keep your arms up. Now, I want you to reach even higher! Now, I want you to reach even higher! Now, if you found yourself being able to reach higher the second time and third time than you did the first, then that means you've trained yourself to be mediocre. I first told you to reach to your highest potential and you didn't. You had an extra inch of effort to give. That's what this chapter is all about. Deciding, takes a made up mind that you will give your absolute best effort, no matter how you feel. You have to decide to go hard no matter what's jumping off in your life at the time.

Step one to completing any task is to first decide! Decide that this is happening. Decide that you're going to take steps toward becoming something different. It's time to execute and without execution there can be no success. One common misconception people have about life is that one day, you will wake up and "everything will magically fall into place" or that time will just magically make everything come together for them. That is NOT TRUE! Nothing will happen for you if you don't make it happen. You can pray all day and night. Hear me, when I tell you that God does not waste answered prayers on the lazy. Most people miss out on there true success because they think it comes with a fancy car and a nice house. When it really comes with a broom and dustpan! If you're not willing to create the circumstances, then you'll be a victim of them. We live in a world where knowledge and understanding are more available than any other time. Our Grandparents and our parents had to work so much harder than we do, yet their generations accomplished so much more! We complain and complain, so much about what we can't do and what we don't have that we don't even realize that we have the world literally at our fingertips! A switch has to go off inside you that makes you decide that you're not going to live life like this anymore. You're not going to be in this same space next year. Throw your vision boards in the trash. You simply have to get better.

When we decide, we decide based on circumstances. For instance, if you walked outside to your car and noticed a growling pit bull staring back at you, you'd probably jump on top of the car or try to take off running in fear. However, if you walked outside and this same pit bull was growling at you, yet this time you had your baby with you then everything changes. You see, the circumstances would instantly change your role from victim to protector. You still have the same chance at getting bitten, but you're not letting your child get harmed. You have to do your goals the same way. Only this time the pit bull is every negative thought and doubtful thing you tell yourself and your baby is your goal that you have to protect. In other words, you have to protect yourself from yourself. Change the circumstances in your mind from I can to I MUST! You have to do this every-single day or you'll eventually slack off. Roll your sleeves up and get your butt to work.

CHAPTER 9: WHY?

You have to have a strong why because your opposition will be just as strong.

9

To me, the word, "why" is the most important word in the English language. This word seals life for us. It wakes us up. It develops us. It pushes us. It hurts us. It scares us. It frustrates us. But at the end of the day, it's why you're reading this. Your why may be different from mine; mine is my son, my legacy and what I leave behind for him. Yours may be for other reasons, but whatever the reason is, it has to be big enough to make you keep going. It has to push you when you feel like giving up. It has to propel you through the toughest seasons of your life. It's the only barrier between you and failure.

I've been on welfare before. I've been evicted before. I've had cars repossessed. I've started businesses that failed. I've been fired from jobs. I've been heartbroken. I've been humiliated. I've been under pressure. But, the only things that kept me from throwing in the towel was that one day I would stare my son in the face and tell him I gave up. If you've found yourself giving up a lot lately, maybe it's because your "why" isn't big enough.

Revisit what's important to you. Look at the life you have and compare it to the life that you desire for yourself. Your value system has to be bigger than a fancy car, a banging body and a nice house. What makes you tick? What gets you out of the bed in the morning? What keeps you going when you have nothing else to rely on? You have to have a strong why because your opposition will be just as strong. I can't tell you how many days that I don't feel like waking up to do a 12 hour shift. Sometimes I wake up, look around the room and I like many of you I have the "man. I want to stay in bed" thoughts. Then, I think about all of the people who need me to get up and be myself. My son thinks I'm a superhero and I wake everyday trying to live up to what he thinks me to be. That's really it, that's my why. I go hard for the people I love and I refuse to let them struggle.

Tonight, I want you to sit and think about what your "why" is. If you can't identify it, then pray to God and He'll show you in time. Let Him reveal it.

CHAPTER 10:
How to Have Faith

If God showed it to you, then stop second guessing yourself.

10

What is Faith? Here's my definition, it's taking steps in a dark room using God's voice to feel your way. Faith is the most-sure and unsure place you'll ever be, at the same time. Faith is so important as you're chasing your goals because there's a good chance you won't make it. There's a good chance that what you're hoping for won't come true. Faith is a tool God uses to link our belief in His power to the choices we make. He understands that there are some things we're just too weak to do alone, so, He created a thing called faith. Faith is like a muscle you build up over time from trusting Him over and over again. Faith is weak in the beginning, and when you see God start to make good on what He promised you, it gets easier to trust Him next time He tells you to do something.

The first time God told me to open up a gym, I sat in the car with my realtor in the front of that building and I cried. This was the most money I had saved up and now God was telling me to spend it all and jump into something totally new. I kept telling my realtor, "I don't know if I'll be able to afford it. The rent is $600.00 a month alone and I'm just now able to pay my rent at home comfortably". This is why you have to have saved people who know God around. My realtor replied. "John, God isn't going to let you go backward. Either you move forward with Him or you walk backwards by yourself". I listened to her. I got out of the car and wrote my first months' deposit to the building owner. After all the success I had seen in that building, two years later, God spoke again. This time He told me to start packing up the gym, then He gave me a date that I was going to move, August 1st 2017, or as I like to say, 8:1. The next day my pastor gets up and preaches about new beginnings. His text was Genesis 8:1. When God confirms that he's with you, there's no reason to doubt yourself or his word. So, this time my faith muscle was a lot stronger. So, I was like "Okay, God let's go!"

The next week I walked to the beauty supply which was next door to the gym and the owner said, "Hey John. I'm looking to leave soon and I want you to have this place. It's on the market for $200,000." At the time I only had $105,000 in the bank. I quickly replied. "Mike, I ain't got that!", I bought my hair stuff and left out. That next day I was in my office alone and he walked in. "Hey John, I know you don't have the $200,000 but do you have $100,000?" I said, "Man, yeah I can do that, but I got to keep stuff rolling here. I can't give you the full $100,000 right now, but I can give you a $50,000 down and I can't pay you until I open up in January, because I need the other $55,000 I have for renovations and payroll." He said, "Okay, no problem. So, when do want to make your first down payment?" I said, "How's 8/1?" He agreed and the building was mine.

God had confirmed his word in less than a months' time. My brother always says "when it's God, you don't have to work it- it just works." If God showed it to you, then stop second guessing yourself. If it's your vision, then it's your assignment. Vision board parties aren't for real visionaries. A vision isn't a wish list, it's a clear instruction only God can give. Always remember that

He only sends the signs to those who are willing to work. He reveals plans and visions when he sees that you're serious about what you're believing Him for. I told you earlier that God doesn't waste blessings on the lazy.

You have some people who wake up and pray asking God to send provision and direction and He's probably saying, "I did! I'm just waiting on you to go look for the building." We want God to show us His plans for us when we don't have any desire to plan anything at all. "God please take me to the bank and drop me off. Tell the bank tellers I'm coming to apply for a business loan and then tell her to approve it. And then I need to come pick me back up and drop me back at home, in Jesus name, Amen." IT DON'T WORK LIKE THAT! You pray for direction, you receive instruction, then you write the vision, and you start working towards it! Stop calling your laziness faith in the future. Faith has legs and they move. If you have a desire to do something but you're too afraid to fail, then your failure has become your new God and fear of failure has never made anyone rich.

CHAPTER 11: SHUT UP!

Never forget that doubt has a voice.

11

Stop self-sabotaging! Sometimes we lose simply because we keep telling ourselves the wrong things. I remember the first time I was on the news. I had built up so much nervousness that when the time came, I had no courage at all. At the beginning of the shoot, I had so much going on in my head that I seriously could not hear the instructions that the Newscaster was giving me. The entire time she was giving me queues and direction, I just stared at her. I literally had to tell myself to SHUT UP! Now when I commanded the doubtful voices in my head, the courage in me looked around at everything I had built. I knew in that moment that I deserved to be where I was. Never forget that doubt has a voice. Stop giving it a platform in your mind. Sometimes our biggest hater is ourselves! Think about it. How many times have you talked yourself onto the ledge to jump only to talk yourself back off? We miss so many opportunities in life because of what we're afraid people will think.

This week, any time you start to doubt yourself or start having thoughts that make you question your worth, stop yourself in your tracks and tell yourself, SHUT UP! So, when you tell yourself, "I can't eat right", SHUT UP! "What if they don't hire me", SHUT UP! "What if I don't get approved for the loan", SHUT UP! Just shut up and go be great. New practice, from now on anytime you have a negative thought start to brew in your head, I want you to say, SHUT UP, out loud. I want you say it no matter where you are, unless you're at church and your Pastor is preaching.

CHAPTER 12:
What If

What if your idea actually works?

12

Everything big started with these two words. One day someone thought, what if we made a car run by electric power? What if we had a phone that could video call? As good as the ideas were, they still had to gather resources and just go for it.

You won't succeed at everything. Now, before I started my own gym, I had a security business. It was called Fortified Security. It was terrible and I never made any money from it. A lot of people don't even know that. They judge me by Grindtime's success and think I've always had it like this. Sometimes, people judge you for your highlight reels, without looking at all the stats you had in the game. Now, even though I didn't make money with Fortified Security, it did look good enough on my resume' to get me hired as a hotel housekeeper, I was making $10.00 an hour. It helped me take care of my responsibilities as a man to take care of myself and my son, while I still built my business. Even as I'm writing this book, I didn't even know if anyone would buy it let alone want to read it. It's my first book and no I didn't have all the answers, but you know what? I tried! And now you've purchased it and it's helping you! I love the saying that says "you miss 100 percent of the shots that you don't take". There's a 100 percent chance that your idea will fail. And there's also a 100 percent chance that your idea will work. It all depends on how much courage you can muster up in the process.

Your will is what separates you from the pack. It doesn't matter how good your idea is. If you don't launch it, you'll never see what it could've been. Many times people are afraid to move on their idea because of what other people may think. But, it's funny how the people we're afraid to be embarrassed in front of aren't even doing anything themselves! If God gives you a vision or a dream, then that means he must trust YOU enough to carry it out. Remember that He doesn't give us anything he doesn't have intentions on helping us to sustain. I remember when I got my first gym facility, I called my mom in such excitement.

She answered the phone and I immediately blurted out, "Mom! I got my building!"
She said "that's good baby. How much have you made so far?"
"Well mom, I've made about $12,000 in last 5 months. And that's just from me training people outside in the park", I said.
"That's good baby, but I think you should wait until you've seen your first $100,000 before you think about getting a building", she replied.

Looking back, I understand that as a mother, she wanted to protect me from any heartbreak or disappointment, as any mother should. However, in that moment, I held the phone crushed and confused. So, I had to make a choice. Listen to my mother and follow her advice or ignore her and try it anyway. I hung up the phone and called the landlord and said, "I'll be there to bring my down payment. I had $13,500 to my name and with all the hope I had left, I spent it all on the renovations. I spent over $11,000 in renovations. I remember at opening day, January 9, 2015 I had $300.00 left to my name. In the midst of 70 people I stood and cried at my grand opening. They thought these were tears of joy, but they were tears of fear. I was scared out of my mind. With only 8 consistent clients, I stood nervous and unaware of what the future would hold. Every doubtful thought that you can think of crossed my mind. With God's direction I put my head down and built my business one client at a time.

I literally gave it everything I had. I made $108,000 that year, I couldn't believe it. My second year I doubled that and expanded again. My third year I had to expand again and bought a 7000 sq. ft. two floor facility. I opened the first black owned fitness center in Detroit. I'm not saying this to boast, I'm saying this to let you know that it's possible! And sometimes you have to ignore all the outside noise, family members, opinions, and advice; and tell yourself you know what, "what if"?

What if you succeed?
What if your business blows up like mine did?
What if your book makes you a household name in the country?
What if your small idea becomes a big blessing to millions?
You'll never know unless you take the shot.

Questions:

1. What are some big goals you have?

2. Why are you so afraid to really try?

CHAPTER 13:
Rest.
Don't Procrastinate.

Stop thinking your goal is a place, the goal is the mindset.

13

One of the best lessons I've learned this year is the benefit of stopping. We can become so next level driven that we'll drive ourselves into the ground trying to "become". When is the last time you stopped for a second just to pat yourself on the back for everything you've accomplished? It's okay to rest for a second and replenish yourself. Even your phone has times where it acts up and the only way to fix it is to turn it off for a second. However, there's a BIG difference in rest and procrastination. YOU DON'T HAVE TIME TO WASTE! Stop listening to people who have never built anything who tell you, "aww baby, you've got all the time in the world" YOU DONT! A lot of people confuse waiting with procrastination, they're very different. Even while you're waiting on your big moment you should be preparing for it. Remember that everything has an expiration date, even your goals. There will be a time when they are unachievable, but if procrastinate too long you'll never get there.

I used to think the longer you waited to open a bottle of wine, the better it would be. I learned that's not true. Wine is a living thing it ages just like us. You see there is a specific time you're supposed to open that bottle of wine to where it's at its peak time. If you don't open it at its peak time, it will eventually sour away. Your goals are the same way. My question to you is what are you refusing to open up inside yourself? What are you talking yourself out of? What do you keep putting off?

Your comfort zone feels good to you right now, but it will eventually kill you. While you're in your comfort zone, someone is out here killing you in private. While you're enjoying every weekend with your friends drinking and partying, someone is strategizing the next 3 moves. While I'm at it, did you know, your weekend makes up 28 percent of your year. If you waste every weekend, then over a span of 10 years, that will equate to about 3 years of wasted time. It's important to know that there is no neutrality in life; either you're moving forward or you're moving backward. Stop thinking your goal is a place, the goal is the mindset. If you can manage to change your mind about an idea, you can change your outcome.

I created the 10 million-minute theory a couple years back and it keeps me in check every time I feel like I have time to waste. The span of 20 years equates to a little over 10,500,000 minutes. Of those 10,500,000 minutes we have to factor in rest and sleep. So, that's about 6 to 8 hours, which takes about 3 million minutes away and that's on the low end. Then the average person spends about 8 to 12 hours at work, which takes away another 3 to 5.5 million of those minutes away. Then we have to factor in responsibilities such as grocery store runs, barbershop and hair appointments, school, family time etc. that all takes away another few million minutes. So, I believe the average person only spends 500,000 to 3 million minutes out of 20 years being able to build a new business, relax, be on a vacation, or to just enjoy sitting on the couch watching their favorite show. This is why balancing your grind is so important.

We don't have as much time as we think, we have to set

our families up. By the time you look up, you're knocking on 50 and it'll time to wind it down. I'm not telling you to work yourself into the ground until you're no good. That's not a good idea. I'm simply telling you to create a healthy balance that allows you to do both. Remember that balance isn't something you find. It's something you've got to create. You can only create it if you have structure which we talked about earlier in this book. When it's time to focus on your family, GIVE THEM THAT TIME! When it's time to work on your business, GIVE YOUR BUSINESS THAT TIME! When it's time to work on your body, GIVE YOUR BODY THAT TIME! Time is not something we can get back. It's okay to rest. Just don't confuse rest with procrastination. When it's your time to die and go to heaven, you have to lie on something called a death bed. You were never meant to live every day on it.

CHAPTER 14:
The Racehorse Approach

I'm on my own path.

14

When it comes to your journey, take the racehorse approach. Racehorse trainers put blinders on their horses during races to keep the horse focused on what's in front of them. It doesn't make the racehorse run any faster. It just keeps the horse from being distracted by what's around it. They run a cleaner path when they focus on what's in front of them. Can you imagine what the winning horse's perspective must look like? They see nothing, but a clear and open path. That's how you have to see yourself everyday. Everyday is a new opportunity on an open path. You can only lose if you chose to compete and you can only compete if you measure yourself to the next person. That will often times discourage you or give you a false sense of where you are.

We're living in a social media dominated culture and if you're not careful you'll compare yourself and your journey to someone else's. What you don't see is that person you're idolizing on social media probably started a year before you did. What you don't see is the mental and emotional battles that-that person has to push through on a daily basis. You don't know if they have peace of mind, you're just focused on that they have a nice car. No one posts their failures, they only post their highlight reels. So, don't get caught up in the hype of what someone else is doing. If you're trying to lose weight, getting frustrated with someone else's fast results isn't going to help you. All you can do is what you can do. And if you're giving yourself your absolute best effort, then you should be satisfied and proud of that. As a matter of fact, you won't even have time or strength to be on social media all day. People who are really, truly building something don't have time to come down off there ladder to come look at someone else's progress. During my really busy seasons at the gym, I rarely have time to even glance at my phone. Especially, if it's to look at what's going on at other gyms on social media.

Looking at other people's progress just slows yours down. Now, it's good to get inspiration from others. I definitely do that from time to time, watching other bodybuilders and seeing what's going in business for other people. However, I don't compare myself to them, there's no reason for me to. I'm on my own path when it comes to my businesses, my family, my body and my walk with God. Keep your journey special by keeping it yours.

My mother and father have been married for almost 40 years now. Neither of them have ever stepped out on one another and as their son, that makes me proud. The reason they've been able to keep it together like that is because they realize how special they are to each other. It'll always be someone stronger or more pretty or taller. However, there will never be another them, that's how you should look at your journey. None of us are perfect, that's what makes us all so great.

Your business journey is going to be different than mine. My fitness journey is different from yours. Wherever you are, just give YOUR best effort.

CHAPTER 15: What's on the "Next Level?"

Be ready to give, give, give.

15

A growing desire nowadays is getting to the next level. Man, oh man let me tell you, the higher I go, the more I miss level one! Let me be the first to tell you that nothings up here but more work! More discipline, more money to invest. So be careful what you're asking for.

There was a time where I could go anywhere, do anything, act any kind of way and no one would bat an eye. Now, I can't even go to a local grocery store without someone noticing me. Sometimes I'm out and people won't say a word to me, but will know exactly who I am. I can't be rude to a waitress. I can't voice every opinion I have on social media because when you have a big platform everyone is watching. So, as soon as I leave my house I'm "ON". As my business grows there's a need for more policies and new staff and more taxes to pay. It's one thing to get to the top but it's another thing to stay there. I always have to be extremely attentive to detail. When I get time to myself it's only a matter of time before I have to clock back in and handle something. To whom much is given, much is required, so, it's no use in me complaining about it. So, this chapter is especially for my entrepreneurs and aspiring business owners out there.

Be ready to give, give, give! If you want to be in business so, you won't have to work for someone else then stay in your cubicle! Entrepreneurship is ONLY about giving and working for others. It's not for the faint of heart. I don't get to have bad days.

Motivation is an Inside Job

I only get to have bad moments, and then I have to shake myself and clock back in mentally and emotionally. There are some days where you have to fake it until you make it. That's a skill that only the strong ones develop. As your level expands, your perspective must expand as well. Your life's level will always be determined by the mental level you're on. Every time I hire someone new I take on the responsibility of feeding their family. Do you know that if I hire someone and then I lose my business or get in trouble and lose everything then someone's kids won't eat? That's pressure, but I chose to take on that pressure every day, but it's pressure nonetheless.

You have to consider everything on the level that you're trying to get to. In all your getting, get an understanding. You want to be a homeowner then be ready for mortgage, taxes, furnace issues and lawn maintenance as well. You can't live in a home with an apartment mindset. You want to own a business? Well be ready for unlimited hours, giving up weekend partying, date nights with your girlfriend or your boyfriend and the occasional call-in sick days. You want to get in shape? Get ready to consistently eat right and drink water instead of sweets and wine at night. Be prepared for muscle soreness from your workouts. You can't expect to build a life worth living without putting in the necessary sacrifices. In the next chapter we'll talk about how to stay focused during the time of sacrifice.

CHAPTER 16:
Pizza vs. Oatmeal

Sacrifice now, enjoy later.

16

Okay, so here we go. The inevitable door that we must all walk through to get to the desired end is called, sacrifice. We always hear about sacrifice and success going hand in hand. But how? How do I change my mind from giving in to short term pleasures to get to a life full of long term happiness? I'm glad you asked. It's simple, Pizza vs Oatmeal.

Imagine this, you're starving for food and you're hungry as ever. You walk in the kitchen and you see two options. One with a bowl of oatmeal and the other with a plate of pizza. The way your body works is that when it's full, it's full. So, both options will achieve the same short term goal, they will get you full. Now while this is true, the pizza will obviously be more enjoyable on the way down your digestive system. However, they both have two totally different long term effects. The pizza will make you fat and the oatmeal will keep your heart healthy and give a you good source of fiber for your day. You have to carry the same mindset into your daily life.

Don't let short term pleasures kill you. Most times short term pleasures lead to long term deterioration; simply because it feels so good at the moment that you can't see how bad it's killing you. You may feel better holding that $200.00 in your account instead of paying that bill, but it's not going to go away! It's only going to get worse if you keep ignoring it, it's going to look bad on your credit and then it's going to go to collections. And it's all because you wanted a pair of shoes instead of being responsible. Life is the same way. Do what you have to do, when you don't want to, or else you'll live a life that you don't want to because you didn't capitalize when you had the chance to. Sacrificing isn't always fun. So, make sure you pack your patience in your bag along your journey. Long term results will be given from long term sacrifices. We want everything to happen so quick for us these days.

This microwaveable success is a myth. You didn't just eat bad for one week and gain 50 pounds. So, you can't expect to just eat clean for one week and lose it either. The business you started may have potential, but what is potential without sacrifice? NOTHING!

Lebron James was always going to be tall. He had to sacrifice the time to learn how to dribble and shoot though. The next time that you're met with an option to go the opposite direction of your goals, remember what the long term effect looks like. Just stay focused and eat the oatmeal. Pay the bill. Drink the water. Do the Workout. Apologize to your spouse. Accept the correction. It'll make you stronger and more responsible in the end.

It's funny how any time life gets tough we blame the devil. When it's probably just a mismanagement of priorities. Your ability to understand a thing determines your ability to keep it. If you don't understand how money works, you won't keep it for very long. If you don't understand how business works, you won't be in business for very long. If you don't understand how marriage is supposed to work, you won't be married very long. Here's how this works, if you want something you make sacrifices to get it, and then you make even bigger sacrifices to keep it. Sacrifice now, enjoy later.

CHAPTER 17:
Be a FINISHER

Drop the weight inside yourself.

17

What if I told you that the way to finish is to not focus on finishing it. I know this sounds crazy, so, just hear me out. I want you to close your eyes. No peeking! Now imagine your dream body. Imagine yourself being at your goal weight, right now. Imagine yourself in that dress that you want to fit into. Fellas, I want you to imagine your arms and chest looking exactly how you want them to look. Imagine that stomach shrinking until you can start to see your abs. Now open your eyes. Do you know that what you just imagined did absolutely NOTHING FOR YOU! Thinking about the finish line doesn't get you any closer to it. Just focus on putting one foot in front of the other and eventually you'll get there. No matter what race you're trying to finish, it can only be won one step at a time. It's good to desire a finished product. It's better to create a disciplined mind and lifestyle to assure a finished product.

We live in a name it and claim it world these days. Where everyone thinks that if you just see it in your mind, it will just magically happen for you. While vision for your future is important, it means nothing without a disciplined lifestyle and work ethic. You can see yourself in that million-dollar house all you want. If you don't build your credit, and save your money, you'll never live in it. Results are just your desires meeting up with your work ethic and consistency. No matter how much you see your body changing in your mind, if you're not willing to eat right, your vision will just be an imagination and it will never happen. I know this isn't the normal ear tickling talk that you usually hear from motivational books and sources. That's exactly what I wanted. I'm tired of people selling you crap that have never been through anything. I want you to stop buying every book that comes out trying to help you fix your life and just look in the mirror and fix YOUR life. It's going to be tough and It's going to be frustrating at times. You can either suffer the pain of discipline or suffer the pain of regret.

      I used to be a motivational junkie myself. In 2015 I lost my focus and I gained 40 pounds. I thought that I needed a million self help books to get my mind back on track, so I would get on the treadmill everyday and listen to every audiobook and watch motivational videos to fuel me for my workout. While it worked at first, it eventually did more harm than good. I noticed myself not giving 100 percent unless I had, *the right video.* One day my phone died right before I got on that treadmill and I just stopped. See I had become so addicted to hearing other people tell me to get my life together. In that moment I decided not only to workout anyway, but to go even harder. During my run, I remember having a deep conversation with myself. I talked to myself about continuing to run. I talked to myself about never getting back to where I spiraled out from. I kept this going every single day and I dropped the weight inside myself; that's what this entire book is about. Applying yourself to yourself.

      There will be negative thoughts that come along the way. That's not always the devil, sometimes it's you. It's you telling yourself that you're not good enough. That you're not worthy or capable enough. That you won't make it this time because you failed the last time. That is all a lie. You can make it. You can live up to your full potential. You can lose the weight. You can build the business. You can fix your marriage. You can raise your kids by yourself. You can finish school. You can stop drinking. You can stop stress eating. You can stop smoking. You can do whatever you put your heart and mind to. You just have to be willing put the effort in. Motivation is an inside job.

FINAL REMARKS and Thank You's

As redundant as it may sound, I want to Thank God. I thank God for creating me. I want to thank Him for every storm that I had to fight through. Every valley that He put me in.

I want to thank God for my pastor, Pastor Welton, who is also my brother. Thank you for giving me really the spiritual foundation that I have now. I want to thank my father for making me the man that I am. I want to thank my mother for showing me how to treat a real woman. I want to thank my son for giving me a reason to pull purpose out of me.

I want to thank everyone who didn't believe in me, this book is for you. I want to thank every job that fired me. If it wasn't for you I probably would've never started my business.

I want to thank every client who ever believed in me, especially the ones that stuck with me when I was just starting. This book is for you too. I want to thank everyone who bought this book. I hope it helps you become the best version of yourself, whether it's physically, mentally, emotionally, financially, or even spiritually.

John Smith

Lastly, I want to thank my heart. I will never stop giving you my best as long as you keep beating.

Notes

John Smith

Notes

Notes

John Smith

Notes

Notes

John Smith

Notes

Notes

Made in the USA
Columbia, SC
05 November 2020